THE COST OF THE ANOINTING

PASTOR DR. CLAUDINE BENJAMIN

Published by:

Editor: Cleveland O. McLeish (Author C. Orville McLeish)

ISBN: 978-1-965635-77-3 (paperback)

TABLE OF CONTENTS

ABOUT THE AUTHOR

Pastor Claudine Benjamin is a passionate voice in this generation—a servant-leader, teacher, and prophetic intercessor called to raise up disciples, ignite the fire of revival, and restore honor to the altar of God. With a heart deeply burdened for truth, holiness, and the presence of God, she carries a message that pierces the heart and awakens the soul to the reality of the cross, the call of consecration, and the power of the anointing.

Her journey has not been one of ease, but one marked by surrender, sacrifice, and a deep personal encounter with the refining fire of God. Pastor Claudine does not write from theory—she writes from the furnace. Her messages and books are birthed through seasons of crushing, silence, obedience, and divine preparation. As a result, her voice carries weight, her words carry oil, and her ministry carries the unmistakable imprint of the Holy Spirit.

She is the author of several spiritually impactful works, each one a prophetic call to return to God's original design for the church— where purity, purpose, and power flow not from personality, but from a life laid down. Through preaching, teaching, writing, and mentoring, she equips believers to walk in divine authority while remaining anchored in humility and submission to the will of God.

Pastor Claudine is also the founder of a ministry that equips leaders, heals the wounded, restores the broken, and prepares the Bride of Christ for His soon return. Her life's mission is to make Jesus known, exalt the Word of God, and raise up a generation who understands that the anointing is not a performance—it is a price.

She lives a life of prayer, worship, and obedience, and remains fully committed to fulfilling the call of God with integrity, honor, and faithfulness. Whether in the pulpit, at the altar, or through the written word, Pastor Claudine Benjamin continues to be a vessel through whom the oil of God freely flows.

"The oil is costly, but the obedience is worth it."

ACKNOWLEDGMENT

With deep gratitude and humility, I pause to acknowledge the many hearts and hands that have contributed to the birth of this book. The Cost of the Anointing was not written in isolation—it was formed through prayer, sacrifice, spiritual support, and the divine orchestration of God through people He placed in my life.

First and foremost, I give all glory, honor, and praise to my Lord and Savior, Jesus Christ. You are the Anointed One, the Lamb that was slain, and the example of ultimate surrender. Every page of this book is a reflection of Your grace, Your calling, and Your Spirit. Thank You for trusting me to carry this message. May every word glorify You and point others toward the altar of true consecration.

To the Holy Spirit—my Teacher, Comforter, and Counselor—thank You for every whisper in the stillness, every revelation in the Word, and every moment of correction and conviction that shaped these pages. Without Your presence, there would be no oil, no insight, and no anointing.

To my family—thank you for your unwavering love, prayers, and patience. Your encouragement gave me strength when the burden of the message felt heavy. You have walked with me through seasons of crushing, and your faith helped carry me through. I honor you for your support, and I thank God for placing you in my life.

To my spiritual covering and mentors—thank you for pouring into my life with wisdom, discipline, and prophetic vision. You have helped shape me, not just as a writer or minister, but as a submitted vessel before the Lord. Your example has taught me the value of hiddenness, the necessity of holiness, and the power of a surrendered life.

To the faithful prayer warriors who lifted me up during the writing of this book—thank you. You covered me when I was weary, and your intercession created an atmosphere for revelation to flow. You may never fully know how vital your role has been, but heaven has recorded your sacrifice.

To every believer who has walked through fire, endured seasons of silence, and continued to say "yes" to God when it would have been easier to quit—this book acknowledges you. Your obedience in obscurity is not in vain. You are the evidence that the anointing still costs something in this generation.

To the editors, designers, and publishing partners—thank you for your excellence, patience, and partnership in bringing this message to life. You helped shape the vision into a finished work, and your attention to detail made the message clearer and stronger.

Lastly, to every reader—thank you for opening your heart to receive what the Lord desires to say through these pages. My prayer is that this book will not only inform you, but transform you. May it draw you deeper into the presence of God, and may it inspire you to count the cost, embrace the process, and pursue the anointing with holy reverence.

From the depths of my heart—thank you.

To God alone be all the glory.

DEDICATION

To the ones who chose the altar over applause—This book is prayerfully and lovingly dedicated to every servant of God who has chosen the hidden path of consecration over the glamorous path of popularity. To those who have labored in secret, cried in silence, and worshipped in the wilderness while the world looked elsewhere—you are not forgotten by God.

To the intercessors who travail in the midnight hour with no audience but heaven.

To the preachers who prepare sermons from a place of brokenness and pour out oil that came through deep crushing.

To the missionaries and evangelists who gave up worldly comforts to obey the whisper of God.

To the worshipers who minister, not for recognition, but from deep wells of surrender.

To the prophets who have carried the burden of the Lord when it cost them relationships, reputation, and rest.

To the pastors who serve faithfully, even when unseen and uncelebrated.

To the pioneers and forerunners who said "yes" to God when it meant walking alone.

This is for every soul who discovered that the anointing does not come cheap. For those who have endured rejection, spiritual warfare, betrayal, hardship, and seasons of isolation, not because you were forgotten, but because you were being forged in the fire of divine preparation.

To the crushed, the tested, the refined—this book is for you. You are proof that the anointing is not about elevation, but about consecration. It is not about public glory, but about private obedience. You understand that while many admire the oil, few will embrace the process that produces it.

May you find strength in these pages. May your journey be validated. May your scars speak of survival, your tears of transformation, and your sacrifice of significance. You carry something holy. You have paid a price. And heaven has taken note.

Above all, this book is dedicated to the Anointed One—Jesus Christ—the perfect example of surrendered obedience. The One who bore the greatest cost that we might be reconciled, redeemed, and anointed to walk in purpose. To Him be all the glory, forever and ever.

> **"But we have this treasure in earthen vessels, that the excellency of the power may be of God, and not of us."**
> **—2 Corinthians 4:7 (KJV)**

INTRODUCTION

THE COST OF THE ANOINTING

There is a weight to the anointing—a sacredness that cannot be fabricated, imitated, or earned by natural means. It is the tangible evidence of God's hand resting upon a life. The anointing is not mere emotionalism or performance; it is the enabling power of the Holy Spirit that equips believers to do the will of God with supernatural effectiveness and spiritual authority. Yet what many admire from a distance, few are willing to pursue, because behind the oil is a crushing. Behind the power is a process. Behind the anointing is a cost.

In an age where platforms are often exalted above altars, and gifting is celebrated more than godliness, the church must be reminded that there is no substitute for the genuine anointing of God. It cannot be purchased with silver or gold, nor can it be attained through shortcuts or superficial dedication. The anointing comes through deep intimacy with God, sacrificial obedience, prolonged seasons of crushing, and a life fully surrendered to the Master's use.

Jesus Himself modeled this truth. Though He was the Son of God, He was led by the Spirit into the wilderness to be tested before beginning His public ministry (see Matthew 4:1). His anointing came with isolation, hunger, spiritual warfare, and complete submission to the will of the Father. Luke 4:18 records Him declaring, **"The Spirit of the Lord is upon me, because he hath anointed me..." (KJV).** But that declaration came after the wilderness. It came after He endured the process. And so it will be with every anointed vessel—before the oil flows, the olive must be crushed.

David was anointed as a young shepherd boy, but he did not ascend to the throne overnight. He endured years of rejection, hiding in caves, fleeing from Saul, and learning to trust God in obscurity. It was in the wilderness—not the palace—where David learned the weight of the anointing. He could have taken shortcuts, but he knew that the call of God must not be fulfilled outside God's timing and process. As Psalm 89:20-21 says, **"I have found David my servant; with my holy oil have I anointed him: With whom my hand shall be established: mine arm also shall strengthen him." (KJV).**

Joseph dreamed of rulership, but before he wore the robe of authority in Egypt, he wore the garments of a slave and a prisoner. The anointing to govern came through betrayal, misunderstanding, waiting, and faithfulness in forgotten places. Psalm 105:18-19 says of him, **"Whose feet they hurt with fetters: he was laid in iron: Until the time that his word came: the word of the Lord tried him." (KJV).** The cost of the anointing on Joseph's life was his willingness to remain submitted and pure, even when every natural circumstance told him otherwise.

We often desire the outcome of the anointing without embracing the pathway that leads to it. We want to carry the oil without enduring the crushing, but the Lord is looking for vessels that have been emptied of self, purified in the fire, and shaped upon the

14

Potter's wheel. Romans 12:1 exhorts us, **"I beseech you therefore, brethren, by the mercies of God, that ye present your bodies a living sacrifice, holy, acceptable unto God, which is your reasonable service." (KJV).** Sacrifice is the doorway to power.

The anointing is not for personal glory. It is not for display or performance. It is given that God might be glorified, that captives might be set free, that chains might be broken, and that His purposes may be fulfilled on the earth. Isaiah 10:27 declares, **"And it shall come to pass in that day, that his burden shall be taken away from off thy shoulder, and his yoke from off thy neck, and the yoke shall be destroyed because of the anointing." (KJV).** The anointing breaks yokes, not builds brands.

This book is a clarion call to count the cost. It is a summons to forsake the shallow waters of convenience and dive into the depths of surrender. It is for those who will trade fame for fire, applause for altar, and comfort for consecration. It is for those who, like Paul, cry out in Philippians 3:10, **"That I may know him, and the power of his resurrection, and the fellowship of his sufferings, being made conformable unto his death." (KJV).**

Throughout the chapters that follow, we will explore what it truly means to carry the anointing of God. We will walk through biblical examples, spiritual principles, and real-life realities of the process that precedes power. This is not a romanticized journey; it is a refining one. But for those who endure, who press in, who yield fully—there is a reward. Not earthly accolades, but eternal impact. Not temporary platforms, but heavenly power.

As you begin this journey, ask yourself this question: *Am I willing to pay the price for the anointing?* Because while gifts are given freely, the anointing is cultivated through fire. And fire does not just warm—it consumes.

Let this be the season where you not only seek the oil, but also embrace the crushing. For only then will the fragrance of heaven flow from your life in a way that truly transforms the world around you.

KEY SCRIPTURES

- Luke 4:18
- Matthew 4:1
- Psalm 89:20-21
- Psalm 105:18-19
- Isaiah 10:27
- Romans 12:1
- Philippians 3:10

CHAPTER ONE

THE CALL COMES WITH A COST

"Then Jesus said to His disciples, 'If anyone desires to come after Me, let him deny himself, and take up his cross, and follow Me.'" — Matthew 16:24 (NKJV)

THE INVITATION TO MORE

The anointing is not merely a badge of honor or a spiritual decoration—it is a sacred empowerment that comes at a significant cost. While many desire to walk in divine power, few are willing to pay the price. The call of God is weighty, and those whom He anoints must first be willing to surrender everything.

THE ANOINTING IS AN ASSIGNMENT

When David was anointed king in 1 Samuel 16, he was not immediately crowned. Instead, he returned to the fields to serve and be shaped. The oil marked him for greatness, but it also marked the beginning of years of testing, warfare, and hiding.

"Then Samuel took the horn of oil and anointed him... and the Spirit of the Lord came upon David from that day forward." — 1 Samuel 16:13 (NKJV)

God doesn't anoint for applause; He anoints for assignment. With the call comes responsibility—and with responsibility comes spiritual warfare, discipline, and deep dependency on God.

SURRENDER IS THE ENTRY POINT

The anointing begins where self ends. God does not pour oil on altars of pride. He looks for hearts that are bowed low, fully yielded, and emptied of personal agenda.

"I have been crucified with Christ; it is no longer I who live, but Christ lives in me..." — Galatians 2:20 (NKJV)

Many want the anointing but not the death of self that precedes it. But the call to carry the oil is a call to die daily to ambition, comfort, and convenience.

THE CALL WILL COST YOU COMFORT

Elisha was plowing his fields when Elijah found him. After the mantle was thrown on him, Elisha burned his plow and slaughtered his oxen (**see 1 Kings 19:19–21**). He was all in. No turning back.

"So Elisha turned back from him, and took a yoke of oxen and slaughtered them and boiled their flesh, using the oxen's equipment, and gave it to the people, and they ate. Then he arose and followed Elijah, and became his servant." — 1 Kings 19:21 (NKJV)

You cannot step into the new while holding on to the old. The call to the anointing demands a break from the familiar and a trust in the divine.

THE COST IS LIFELONG

The cost of the anointing is not a one-time payment. It is a continual surrender, a consistent sacrifice. Those who carry the oil are often misunderstood, lonely, and called to higher levels of obedience. Yet the reward is intimacy with God, effectiveness in ministry, and eternal impact.

"For everyone to whom much is given, from him much will be required; and to whom much has been committed, of him they will ask the more." — Luke 12:48 (NKJV)

REFLECTION QUESTIONS

- What has God asked you to leave behind in order to walk in your calling?

- Have you truly surrendered all to Him—or are you holding back in certain areas?

KEY TAKEAWAY

The anointing is not free. It costs you your plans, pride, and sometimes your peace, but what you gain in return is the presence, power, and purpose of God.

CHAPTER TWO

BROKENNESS BEFORE POWER

"The sacrifices of God are a broken spirit, a broken and a contrite heart—These, O God, You will not despise." — **Psalm 51:17 (NKJV)**

THE PATHWAY FEW WANT TO WALK

Before there is power, there must be brokenness. Before a vessel can be filled with fresh oil, it must first be emptied. Many want the glory of the anointing but resist the process that produces it. Yet throughout scripture, we see this pattern: God breaks those He intends to use greatly. He crushes the flesh so that the Spirit may reign. He removes self so that His power can rest upon us.

GOD USES THE BROKEN

The world discards the broken, but God chooses them. He does not anoint the perfect; He anoints the surrendered. In fact, brokenness is often God's preparation for elevation.

Consider Joseph—betrayed, enslaved, imprisoned. Yet in the prison of affliction, God was shaping the character that would one day govern a nation.

"But as for you, you meant evil against me; but God meant it for good…" — Genesis 50:20 (NKJV)

The cost of the anointing for Joseph was rejection, pain, and misunderstanding. But through his brokenness, he was entrusted with divine authority.

THE CRUSHING PRODUCES THE OIL

Olive oil doesn't flow until the olive is crushed. Likewise, the anointing only flows through those who have been pressed in secret places—places where pride dies, flesh surrenders, and obedience deepens.

Jesus, the Anointed One, experienced Gethsemane—literally meaning "olive press"—where He sweated drops of blood under pressure. Yet in that moment of crushing, He fully submitted to the Father's will.

"…not My will, but Yours, be done." — Luke 22:42 (NKJV)

True anointing is birthed where there is a full "yes" to God in the midst of great personal cost.

BROKENNESS BIRTHS COMPASSION AND POWER

Those who have walked through pain carry a depth that shallow waters cannot hold. Brokenness produces compassion. When you've been through the valley, you're better able to minister to others with humility and wisdom.

> **"For we do not have a High Priest who cannot sympathize with our weaknesses…"** — Hebrews 4:15 (NKJV)

The power of the anointing is not just for public ministry—it is for private compassion. God entrusts His power to those who will not use it for pride, but for purpose.

God Breaks What He Wants to Multiply

In the miracle of the loaves and fish, Jesus took the bread, blessed it, broke it, and then multiplied it.

> **"And when He had given thanks, He broke it and said, 'Take, eat; this is My body which is broken for you…'"** — 1 Corinthians 11:24 (NKJV)

That same divine principle applies to us. Your brokenness is not the end—it's the beginning of multiplication. God will use your pain to feed others. He will use your story to bring life. But first, He must break what you thought could stay whole.

The Power Comes After the Breaking

After Jacob wrestled with God, he was left with a limp. He was never the same. But it was in that moment of brokenness that his name—and his destiny—was changed.

> **"Your name shall no longer be called Jacob, but Israel; for you have struggled with God and with men, and have prevailed."** — Genesis 32:28 (NKJV)

Brokenness leaves a mark. You may walk with a limp, but you also walk with a new name, a new authority, and a deeper anointing.

REFLECTION QUESTIONS

- What area of your life has God used to break pride or self-dependence?

- Have you allowed God to use your pain for His purpose?

- Are you willing to embrace brokenness as preparation rather than punishment?

KEY TAKEAWAY

The anointing does not fall on the untested—it rests on the broken. Those who have been through the crushing process emerge with oil that is pure, powerful, and purposeful. God cannot fill what is already full. He anoints the emptied, the humbled, and the broken-hearted.

CHAPTER THREE

THE WEIGHT OF THE MANTLE

"Then Elijah passed by him and threw his mantle on him."
— 1 Kings 19:19 (NKJV)

IT'S MORE THAN A SYMBOL

The mantle was not just a garment—it represented the calling, authority, and responsibility of the prophet. When Elijah cast his mantle upon Elisha, it marked a divine transfer, but it also initiated a journey that would require sacrifice, endurance, and faithfulness. The anointing carries glory, but it also carries weight—and that weight is not to be taken lightly.

Many desire the mantle, but few are prepared for its pressure. It requires more than excitement—it requires endurance. The mantle is a burden as much as it is a blessing.

THE MANTLE MARKS YOU FOR SERVICE

Elisha was plowing when the mantle was placed upon him. He immediately knew life would never be the same. The mantle was not just a promotion; it was an invitation to serve.

"So Elisha turned back from him, and took a yoke of oxen and slaughtered them and boiled their flesh, using the oxen's equipment, and gave it to the people, and they ate. Then he arose and followed Elijah, and became his servant." — 1 Kings 19:21 (NKJV)

True anointing doesn't begin in the spotlight. It begins in secret, in surrender, and in service. The mantle identifies, but it also assigns. Elisha stepped from the field into formation. He became a student, a servant, and an observer before he became a miracle-working prophet.

THE MANTLE WILL BE TESTED

Carrying the mantle doesn't exempt you from trials—it invites them. Elijah, though deeply anointed, was often pursued, threatened, and isolated. The weight of the mantle pressed him into places of discouragement and despair.

"But he himself went a day's journey into the wilderness, and came and sat down under a broom tree. And he prayed that he might die, and said, "It is enough! Now, Lord, take my life, for I am no better than my fathers!"" — 1 Kings 19:4 (NKJV)

The weight of the anointing can feel crushing when you're misunderstood, when your obedience leads to isolation, or when you're called to speak truth to a generation that resists it. But these tests are necessary—for they refine the vessel to carry the oil well.

THE MANTLE REQUIRES SEPARATION

The anointing sets you apart. When Elisha accepted the mantle, he burned his plow. He did not leave a backup plan. He left everything behind to follow God's purpose.

> **"No one, having put his hand to the plow, and looking back, is fit for the kingdom of God." — Luke 9:62 (NKJV)**

To carry the mantle means being set apart from the crowd, the common, and the convenient. It may cost you relationships, opportunities, and popularity, but what you gain in return is divine trust and spiritual authority.

THE MANTLE IS TRANSFERRED THROUGH PROCESS

When Elisha asked for a double portion of Elijah's spirit, Elijah didn't simply hand it to him. He said:

> **"You have asked a hard thing. Nevertheless, if you see me when I am taken from you, it shall be so for you; but if not, it shall not be so." — 2 Kings 2:10 (NKJV)**

Elisha had to walk through the process. From Gilgal to Bethel, from Jericho to Jordan, he followed. Every stop tested his loyalty. Every city refined his character. Before the mantle fell, Elisha proved he would carry it with honor.

The anointing is never given casually—it is passed through perseverance, humility, and consistent pursuit.

THE MANTLE IS NOT FOR SHOW—IT'S FOR IMPACT

When Elisha picked up Elijah's mantle, the people didn't immediately accept him. But the moment he struck the Jordan and it parted, they declared:

"The spirit of Elijah rests on Elisha." — 2 Kings 2:15 (NKJV)

The anointing is not validated by titles or garments, but by fruit. The mantle must move heaven and shift the earth. It is not a fashion piece—it's a spiritual force.

REFLECTION QUESTIONS

- Have you counted the cost of the mantle you're praying for?

- Are you willing to serve in hiddenness before walking in authority?

- What comforts or attachments do you need to release to fully follow the call?

KEY TAKEAWAY

The mantle is not a mere symbol—it is a weighty call to represent God with integrity, boldness, and purity. Those who carry it must walk closely with God, die to self, and endure the trials that come with divine responsibility. But for those who carry it well, heaven backs every step.

CHAPTER FOUR

SOLITUDE AND SEPARATION

"But Jesus often withdrew to lonely places and prayed." — Luke 5:16 (NIV)

CALLED APART TO GO DEEPER

O ne of the most misunderstood aspects of the anointing is the role of solitude. Many think that increased anointing brings greater visibility, but often, it brings greater separation. The path to carrying God's presence is marked by seasons of isolation—where the noise of the crowd fades, and the voice of God becomes clear.

The anointed are not only called to something; they are often called away from something. To be set apart by God means to embrace moments of divine solitude, where He becomes your source, voice, and strength.

SEPARATION IS NOT REJECTION—IT'S REFINEMENT

Many anointed vessels confuse divine separation with abandonment. But God does His deepest work in the wilderness. He separates to sanctify. Moses, called to lead a nation, first had to spend forty years in the desert, away from power, reputation, and comfort.

> **"Moses agreed to stay with the man, who gave his daughter Zipporah to Moses in marriage." — Exodus 2:21 (NIV)**

> **"Now Moses was tending the flock... And the angel of the Lord appeared to him in a flame of fire..." — Exodus 3:1–2 (NKJV)**

Before God speaks through you, He speaks to you—often in lonely places. Separation is not punishment; it is preparation.

SOLITUDE TRAINS YOUR EARS TO HEAR GOD

In seasons of solitude, distractions are stripped away. The crowd no longer feeds your identity. The applause disappears. And in that silence, the voice of the Lord becomes distinct.

Jesus often withdrew, not because He lacked ministry opportunities, but because He needed intimacy with the Father.

> **"Now in the morning, having risen a long while before daylight, He went out and departed to a [a]solitary place; and there He prayed." — Mark 1:35 (NKJV)**

The deeper the anointing, the deeper the need for undistracted time with God. Power flows from proximity, not performance.

SEPARATION OFTEN COMES BEFORE ELEVATION

David was anointed by Samuel, but he didn't move immediately to the throne. Instead, he went back to solitude with sheep. His promotion came through private worship, not public recognition.

> **"He also chose David His servant, and took him from the sheepfolds; From following the ewes that had young He brought him, to shepherd Jacob His people, and Israel His inheritance." — Psalm 78:70–71 (NKJV)**

The pasture was David's training ground. The solitude cultivated character, sensitivity to God's voice, and a heart of worship. Before God elevates you, He separates you to shape you.

THE ANOINTING ATTRACTS ISOLATION AND OPPOSITION

The moment the mantle falls, the separation begins. Joseph was set apart by dreams and favor, yet misunderstood and rejected by his own brothers.

> **"Now when they saw him afar off, even before he came near them, they conspired against him to kill him." — Genesis 37:18 (NKJV)**

Rejection and isolation are common for those who carry something divine. The anointing makes you different, and difference invites discomfort in others. But that discomfort becomes your cocoon—a sacred place where God shields, matures, and refines His vessel.

YOU CANNOT CARRY GLORY AND FIT EVERYWHERE

Not everyone can walk where you're going. Some relationships, environments, and conversations must be left behind. God prunes your circle to preserve your calling.

"Come out from among them and be separate, says the Lord. Do not touch what is unclean, and I will receive you."
— 2 Corinthians 6:17 (NKJV)

Holiness is not optional for the anointed. God's oil flows on those who are willing to live set apart, not just in behavior, but in heart posture.

REFLECTION QUESTIONS

- Are you embracing or resisting God-ordained seasons of solitude?

- What habits, people, or places is God calling you to separate from?

- Have you learned to hear God clearly in the quiet?

KEY TAKEAWAY

Solitude is not the absence of purpose—it is the secret chamber of preparation. God separates those He anoints so that their power flows from intimacy, not insecurity. If you're in a season where God has pulled you back, know that He's not finished with you—He's forming you.

CHAPTER FIVE

OBEDIENCE OVER OPPORTUNITY

"To obey is better than sacrifice, and to heed is better than the fat of rams." — 1 Samuel 15:22 (NIV)

THE CHOICE THAT DEFINES THE ANOINTED

Anointing is not maintained by charisma—it is sustained by obedience. There will come moments in your walk when you must choose between what looks like a good opportunity and what God has commanded. These decisions reveal whether you serve the anointing or the platform, whether you value God's presence or people's praise.

Obedience is often costly. It may close doors, delay advancement, or even bring ridicule. But for the anointed, obedience is non-negotiable. God will not pour out oil on rebellion. To carry His power, you must first carry His will, even when it conflicts with your own.

SAUL: WHEN OPPORTUNITY REPLACES OBEDIENCE

King Saul was chosen, anointed, and positioned for greatness. But he lost everything, not because of immorality, but because he chose partial obedience. He sacrificed before God instructed him to. He spared what should have been destroyed. He gave in to pressure rather than obeying God's clear voice.

"Because you have rejected the word of the Lord, he has rejected you as king." — 1 Samuel 15:23 9NIV)

Saul chose what looked right instead of what God said was right. That is the danger of opportunity without discernment. One act of disobedience can cost you the oil.

OBEDIENCE OFTEN LEADS THROUGH THE UNPOPULAR PATH

When God told Noah to build an ark, there was no rain, no storm, no audience—just instructions. For years, he obeyed in silence, mocked by men, but anchored by God's Word.

"Noah did everything just as God commanded him." — Genesis 6:22 (NIV)

Obedience will often make you look foolish. You may be laughed at, misunderstood, or isolated. But obedience opens doors no man can shut. The anointing rides on the back of relentless surrender.

JESUS: THE ULTIMATE EXAMPLE OF COSTLY OBEDIENCE

Jesus didn't avoid the cross—He submitted to it. Though fully God, He humbled Himself and obeyed even unto death.

"And being found in appearance as a man, he humbled himself by becoming obedient to death—even death on a cross!" — Philippians 2:8 (NIV)

The path to resurrection always includes crucifixion. If we want resurrection power, we must embrace crucified obedience. There is no shortcut around it. Every anointed vessel must pass through Gethsemane, whispering, **"Not my will, but Yours be done."**

The anointed must train their ears to hear, not just any voice, but God's voice. Not every open door is divine. Not every invitation is kingdom-sanctioned. Many have lost the anointing by chasing exposure instead of assignment.

"My sheep hear My voice, and I know them, and they follow Me." — John 10:27 (NKJV)

Obedience requires intimacy—because you cannot follow the voice of a God you rarely spend time with. When your direction is rooted in relationship, your obedience becomes clear and unwavering.

The Reward of Obedience Is Fresh Oil

While Saul was losing his anointing through disobedience, David was gaining his through obedience in secret. He worshiped in the fields, protected sheep, and honored leadership, even when that leadership tried to kill him.

"And the Lord said, 'Arise, anoint him; for this is the one!'" — 1 Samuel 16:12 (NKJV)

God looks for obedient hearts—not flashy talent. David was anointed because his heart followed God's commands, even when it hurt. And it was that obedience that attracted the oil.

REFLECTION QUESTIONS

- Have you compromised obedience for opportunity?

- Are you in a season where obedience is costing you something?

- Are you seeking God's will—or justifying your own?

KEY TAKEAWAY

The anointing thrives in the soil of obedience. Every opportunity must be filtered through the question: *"Is this God's will?"* The obedient may be overlooked by man, but they are chosen by heaven. If you want sustained power, obey without hesitation, even when it costs you everything.

CHAPTER SIX

HIDDEN BEFORE HONORED

"He who dwells in the secret place of the Most High shall abide under the shadow of the Almighty." — Psalm 91:1 (NKJV)

BEFORE THE SPOTLIGHT, THERE IS A CAVE

Before God brings you to the palace, He will often lead you through the wilderness. Before you are honored publicly, you will be tested privately. The anointing is not forged in the crowd but in the hidden place—in seasons where you are unseen, uncelebrated, and unnoticed by man, but deeply formed by God.

Every true carrier of the anointing must go through the school of obscurity. It is in the hiding place that God refines character, uproots pride, and teaches dependence. Honor without hiding leads to pride. Hiding before honor creates vessels that can carry the weight of glory.

DAVID: ANOINTED BUT STILL TENDING SHEEP

David was anointed king as a young man, but after the oil flowed, he did not immediately ascend the throne. He went back to feeding sheep and playing his harp in solitude. He was marked by God but forgotten by men.

> **"There remains yet the youngest, and there he is, keeping the sheep." — 1 Samuel 16:11 (NKJV)**

God anointed him while others overlooked him. But it was in the fields that David learned worship, warfare, and integrity. His private victories with lions and bears prepared him for the public victory over Goliath.

Lesson: The hiding place is not a prison—it's a proving ground.

JOSEPH: HIDDEN IN A PRISON BEFORE STANDING IN THE PALACE

Joseph received dreams of greatness, but before the fulfillment came betrayal, slavery, and prison. It seemed like every step forward pushed him deeper into hiding. Yet God was working behind the scenes.

> **"But the Lord was with Joseph in the prison and showed him His faithful love." — Genesis 39:21 (NLT)**

In prison, Joseph's character was tested. His gift was matured. He learned to interpret the dreams of others before his own dreams came to pass.

Lesson: The place of confinement is often the place of consecration.

JESUS: THIRTY YEARS OF SILENCE FOR THREE YEARS OF POWER

The Son of God lived in obscurity for three decades before stepping into public ministry. He was not rushed into influence. Instead, He submitted to the Father's timing.

> **"Jesus grew in wisdom and in stature and in favor with God and all the people." — Luke 2:52 (NLT)**

Even Jesus waited. Even Jesus was hidden. This reminds us that the process of being prepared is more important than the platform of being seen.

Lesson: Don't despise the silence—it's shaping you for the shout.

THE HIDING PLACE IS A PLACE OF INTIMACY

God often hides His anointed ones to cultivate intimacy. It's in the secret place that the flesh dies, motives are purified, and identity is rooted in God alone, not in applause, achievement, or affirmation.

> **"But you, when you pray, go into your room... pray to your Father who is in the secret place; and your Father... will reward you openly." — Matthew 6:6 (NKJV)**

Public power flows from private surrender. God reveals Himself most deeply to those who are content to be with Him when no one else is watching.

WHEN GOD HIDES YOU, HE'S PRESERVING YOU

Sometimes, God hides you for your own protection. He shields you from premature exposure. You may feel forgotten, but in truth, He is preparing you for something greater than you can imagine.

"And made Me a polished shaft; in His quiver He has hidden Me." — Isaiah 49:2 (NKJV)

God is polishing you. You are an arrow in His hand. And when the time is right, He will launch you into purpose.

REFLECTION QUESTIONS

- Are you resisting your season of hiddenness?

- What is God teaching you in the quiet place?

- Do you trust God's timing more than your desire to be seen?

KEY TAKEAWAY

Every anointed vessel must walk through the hidden place. It is there that your roots grow deep, your heart is purified, and your ears are tuned to the whisper of God. Honor without hiddenness is dangerous. But when you've been hidden by God, you emerge not just seen, but ready.

CHAPTER SEVEN

FURNACE-TESTED FAITH

"But He knows the way that I take; when He has tested me, I shall come forth as gold." — Job 23:10 (NKJV)

THE FIRE THAT PROVES THE VESSEL

The anointing is not forged in ease—it is tested in fire. Every vessel called to carry God's glory must endure the furnace of affliction. Not because God is cruel, but because true power must be purified. The oil flows best through vessels that have passed through seasons of intense testing and emerged refined.

Furnace-tested faith isn't fragile. It doesn't break when life does. It doesn't crumble when the promise is delayed. It's faith that's been proven—faith that has wrestled with doubt and come out clinging to God's Word more tightly than ever.

SHADRACH, MESHACH, AND ABEDNEGO: FAITH THAT DOESN'T FLINCH

When these three Hebrew men were commanded to bow to Nebuchadnezzar's golden image or be thrown into the fire, their response revealed the kind of faith God honors.

"If that is the case, our God whom we serve is able to deliver us from the burning fiery furnace, and He will deliver us from your hand, O king. But if not, let it be known to you, O king, that we do not serve your gods, nor will we worship the gold image which you have set up." — Daniel 3:17–18 (NKJV)

They didn't worship with conditions. They had furnace-tested faith—faith that trusts even when the outcome is uncertain.

And in the fire, something remarkable happened: God joined them.

"Look! I see four men loose, walking in the midst of the fire... and the form of the fourth is like the Son of God." — Daniel 3:25 (NKJV)

Lesson: The fire doesn't destroy the anointed—it reveals the God who walks with them.

JOB: FAITH THAT HOLDS ON WHEN EVERYTHING ELSE FALLS APART

Job lost his wealth, health, and children in a matter of moments. His friends accused him, his wife said, **"Curse God and die,"** and yet—he held on.

"Though He slay me, yet will I trust Him." — Job 13:15 (NKJV)

Furnace-tested faith is not always loud or impressive. Sometimes, it's the quiet decision to trust when nothing makes sense.

Lesson: The anointing will attract seasons where your theology is challenged and your foundation is shaken, but what survives the fire is your real faith.

PETER: WHEN FAILURE MEETS REFINEMENT

Peter, bold and anointed, denied Jesus three times in a moment of fear. He wept bitterly. But Jesus was not done with him. His failure became the furnace that refined his faith.

> **"Simon, Simon! Indeed, Satan has asked for you, that he may sift you as wheat. But I have prayed for you, that your faith should not fail; and when you have returned to Me, strengthen your brethren." — Luke 22:31–32 (NKJV)**

Even in the fire of personal failure, God is interceding for His anointed ones. Peter's greatest ministry came after his greatest mistake—because he was restored by fire.

Lesson: Don't mistake fire for rejection. Sometimes, God uses the fire to purge pride and prepare you for greater authority.

FAITH MUST BE TESTED TO BE TRUSTED

You cannot walk in deep anointing with shallow faith. God will lead you into the unknown, ask you to obey without understanding, and stretch your trust until it becomes stronger.

> **"that the genuineness of your faith, being much more precious than gold that perishes, though it is tested by fire, may be found to praise, honor, and glory at the revelation of Jesus Christ." — 1 Peter 1:7 (NKJV)**

God doesn't test you to fail you. He tests you to prove you—to establish a faith that can carry the oil without crumbling under the pressure of ministry, warfare, or temptation.

THE FURNACE PREPARES YOU FOR GREATER FIRE

There's a difference between fire that burns you and fire that builds you. God uses the furnace to create capacity—to deepen your dependence and expand your strength. The greater the anointing, the greater the fire you'll walk through.

But every furnace you pass through becomes fuel for your future ministry. People will be drawn, not to your title, but to the fire you've survived—and the oil that drips from your scars.

REFLECTION QUESTIONS

- What furnace are you currently walking through?

- Are you trusting God in the fire—or trying to escape it?

- Can your faith survive without visible evidence of a breakthrough?

KEY TAKEAWAY

Furnace-tested faith is the kind of faith that heaven can trust. It may bend, but it will not break. It weeps, but it still believes. Those who carry the anointing must walk through the fire, not around it. But in every flame, there is fellowship with the Fourth Man—Jesus, the Faithful One.

CHAPTER EIGHT

THE CRUSHING PRODUCES THE OIL

"I have trodden the winepress alone... I looked, but there was no one to help; Therefore My own arm brought salvation for Me." — Isaiah 63:3, 5 (NKJV)

OIL ONLY FLOWS THROUGH PRESSURE

The anointing is often described as oil, but few understand the process by which oil is produced. It does not flow from the olive until the olive is crushed. There is no shortcut. Crushing is not a metaphorical hardship—it is a real, divinely orchestrated process that God uses to extract purity, power, and purpose from your life.

Everyone wants the oil, but few want the crushing. Yet those who are most anointed are often those who have bled the most in private. If you want to carry fresh oil, you must be willing to walk through the pressing.

GETHSEMANE: WHERE THE ANOINTED IS CRUSHED

Gethsemane means *"oil press."* It is the place Jesus went to pray before the crucifixion—the place of agony, surrender, and deep spiritual anguish.

> **"And being in agony, He prayed more earnestly. Then His sweat became like great drops of blood falling down to the ground." — Luke 22:44 (NKJV)**

The crushing that took place in Gethsemane wasn't physical—it was emotional and spiritual. Jesus wasn't just preparing for death; He was surrendering His will completely.

Lesson: The anointing is not released until your will has been fully crushed by His.

CRUSHED TO RELEASE WHAT'S HIDDEN

The olive looks smooth and whole on the outside, but it contains oil on the inside. That oil doesn't flow through slicing—it flows through pressure.

> **"Most assuredly, I say to you, unless a grain of wheat falls into the ground and dies, it remains alone; but if it dies, it produces much grain." — John 12:24 (NKJV)**

Your full potential cannot emerge until you've allowed God to apply pressure. Hidden inside you is more oil than you realize, but it is released through trials, betrayal, loss, and obedience in pain.

CRUSHING EXPOSES WHAT CAN'T STAY

The crushing not only draws out the oil, but also removes impurities. The flesh of the olive is separated from the oil through heat and weight. Similarly, the crushing in your life will separate flesh from spirit, pride from purity, and show you what is truly within.

> **"For You, O God, have tested us; You have refined us as silver is refined... We went through fire and through water; but You brought us out to rich fulfillment." — Psalm 66:10, 12 (NKJV)**

Lesson: Crushing doesn't just produce—it purifies. The anointing you carry after crushing will be cleaner, deeper, and more sacred.

ANOINTING REQUIRES DEATH BEFORE RESURRECTION

Jesus was crushed, pierced, and buried, but out of His suffering came the resurrection power that now empowers His church.

> **"But He was wounded for our transgressions, He was bruised for our iniquities; The chastisement for our peace was upon Him, and by His stripes we are healed." — Isaiah 53:5 (NKJV)**

You cannot walk in resurrection power until you have endured crucifixion pressure. The crushing must come first. This is why Paul said:

> **"I die daily." — 1 Corinthians 15:31 (NKJV)**

To stay anointed, you must allow God to keep you in a posture of continual surrender and dying to self.

THE OIL AFTER THE CRUSHING IS FOR SERVICE, NOT STATUS

In biblical times, oil was used to anoint kings, priests, and prophets, not for prestige, but for consecration. It wasn't about being admired—it was about being set apart to serve.

"And you shall anoint Aaron and his sons, and consecrate them, that they may minister to Me as priests." — Exodus 30:30 (NKJV)

The crushing teaches humility. After the oil flows, you'll no longer desire the platform—you'll desire God's presence. You'll know the cost of that oil, and you'll never use it to glorify yourself.

REFLECTION QUESTIONS

- What is God trying to produce through your season of pressure?

- Are you allowing the crushing to bring oil—or are you resisting it?

- Do you value what's flowing from your life more than what people see externally?

KEY TAKEAWAY

There is no anointing without crushing. It is painful, personal, and often private—but it is purposeful. What flows from the pressing seasons of your life will nourish others, glorify God, and mark you as a vessel set apart. Don't curse the crushing. It's producing the oil that hell cannot counterfeit and flesh cannot fabricate.

CHAPTER NINE

REJECTION, RIDICULE, AND REFINEMENT

"He was despised and rejected by men, a Man of sorrows and acquainted with grief... and we did not esteem Him."
— Isaiah 53:3 (NKJV)

THE LONELY ROAD OF THE ANOINTED

The anointing often attracts rejection before it brings recognition. Those chosen by God to carry His oil frequently find themselves misunderstood, excluded, criticized, and cast aside, not because they've done wrong, but because of the weight they carry.

Rejection is not the absence of God's hand on your life. In fact, it is often the evidence that His hand is upon you in an uncommon way. The ridicule you endure today may be God's tool for refining you for the elevation you will walk in tomorrow.

JESUS: REJECTED SO YOU COULD BE RECEIVED

Jesus, the Anointed One, experienced ultimate rejection. He was despised by His own people, abandoned by His followers, and crucified by the very ones He came to save.

"He came to His own, and His own did not receive Him."
— John 1:11 (NKJV)

His rejection wasn't a sign of failure—it was the fulfillment of prophecy and the gateway to redemption. If Jesus was rejected, we must understand that rejection will often accompany the mantle we carry.

Lesson: You can be fully in the will of God and still be rejected by people.

DAVID: FROM HERO TO HUNTED

David, after defeating Goliath, was celebrated, but that celebration was short-lived. When Saul heard the praises sung about David, jealousy set in. What followed was years of David being chased, slandered, and hunted like a criminal.

"So Saul eyed David from that day forward. And it happened on the next day that the distressing spirit from God came upon Saul, and he prophesied inside the house. So David played music with his hand, as at other times; but there was a spear in Saul's hand. And Saul cast the spear, for he said, "I will pin David to the wall!" But David escaped his presence twice." — 1 Samuel 18:9–11

David did nothing wrong. He was faithful, loyal, and obedient. Yet he was rejected by the king he served. This is the paradox of the anointing—it draws both favor and fury.

Lesson: The anointing on your life may provoke opposition you didn't ask for. But the wilderness birthed by rejection becomes the womb of refinement.

JOSEPH: RIDICULED FOR A DREAM

Joseph was rejected, not by strangers, but by his own brothers. They mocked his dreams, stripped him of his coat, threw him in a pit, and sold him into slavery.

> **"Look, this dreamer is coming! Come therefore, let us now kill him and cast him into some pit..." — Genesis 37:19–20 (NKJV)**

The anointing on your life may intimidate those who don't understand it. Joseph's dream wasn't arrogant—it was prophetic. But because of it, he endured rejection, betrayal, and isolation. And yet, it was that very path that positioned him for power.

Lesson: Rejection is often redirection. God uses it to put you on a divine path that no man can block.

RIDICULE IS THE FIRE THAT BURNS OFF PRIDE

Every anointed individual must face ridicule—it is the fire that purifies motives. Ridicule keeps us humble, presses us into God, and exposes any desire for validation from people.

When Nehemiah began rebuilding the wall, he faced intense mocking:

> **"What are these feeble Jews doing? Will they fortify themselves? Will they offer sacrifices? Will they complete it in a day? Will they revive the stones from the heaps of rubbish—stones that are burned?" — Nehemiah 4:2 (NKJV)**

But Nehemiah didn't stop. He kept building. He ignored the taunts and fulfilled his assignment. Like Nehemiah, your obedience must outweigh your need for approval.

Lesson: Those who carry the oil must also carry the resolve to build in the face of scorn.

REFINEMENT COMES THROUGH RESISTANCE

Refinement is not comfortable, but it is necessary. The resistance you face is not random. It's forging in you a resilience that can carry responsibility. God will allow rejection to strip you of everything superficial so that your identity is rooted in Him alone.

> **"In this you greatly rejoice, though now for a little while, if need be, you have been grieved by various trials, that the genuineness of your faith, being much more precious than gold that perishes, though it is tested by fire, may be found to praise, honor, and glory at the revelation of Jesus Christ." — 1 Peter 1:6–7 (NKJV)**

God is not refining your talent—He is refining your heart. The furnace of rejection will remove your dependency on applause and replace it with the strength to obey in silence.

REFLECTION QUESTIONS

- Have you experienced rejection because of your obedience or calling?

- Are you allowing ridicule to stop your progress—or refine your purpose?

- What areas of your heart is God trying to purify through opposition?

KEY TAKEAWAY

Rejection is not the enemy of the anointed—it is often the tutor that prepares them for destiny. When people push you away, God is pulling you deeper. When ridicule rises, so does refinement. The fire may feel personal, but it is purposeful. Trust the One who called you, even when others don't.

CHAPTER TEN

SUSTAINED BY GOD ALONE

"My grace is sufficient for you, for My strength is made perfect in weakness." — 2 Corinthians 12:9 (NKJV)

WHEN GOD IS ALL YOU HAVE—AND THAT'S ENOUGH

One of the greatest revelations for the anointed is this: you are sustained by God alone, not by applause, not by support systems, not by connections, nor by titles. The anointing places you in positions where you must lean wholly on God, not as a last resort, but as your only source.

Those who carry the weight of God's presence must first learn to carry the weight of God's dependency. You cannot walk in divine authority while relying on human strength. God will lead you into seasons where He strips everything familiar so you can discover that He is more than enough.

ELIJAH: FED BY RAVENS IN THE DROUGHT

Elijah had just declared a national drought by the word of the Lord. Then God hid him by the brook Cherith—alone—no crowds, no platform, no provision—except what God sent.

> **"The ravens brought him bread and meat in the morning, and bread and meat in the evening; and he drank from the brook." — 1 Kings 17:6 (NKJV)**

This was not punishment—it was training. God was teaching Elijah to rely on Him daily, not on man. The same mouth that called down fire had to first learn to trust God for food.

Lesson: Before God sends you to confront nations, He sends you to the brook—to learn that He alone sustains His servants.

PAUL: STRENGTH IN WEAKNESS

Paul, one of the most anointed apostles in scripture, faced shipwrecks, beatings, imprisonments, and abandonment. And yet, he penned these words from a prison cell:

> **"I have learned both to be full and to be hungry, both to abound and to suffer need. 13 I can do all things through [c]Christ who strengthens me." — Philippians 4:12–13 (NKJV)**

Paul wasn't sustained by a strong ministry team or an ideal environment. He was sustained by Christ. Even when God refused to remove his **"thorn in the flesh,"** Paul learned that divine strength is released in human weakness.

"...when I am weak, then I am strong." — 2 Corinthians 12:10 (NKJV)

Lesson: The anointing is most evident, not in your strength, but in how deeply you trust God when everything else is stripped away.

JESUS: ALONE IN THE WILDERNESS

Before Jesus launched into public ministry, the Spirit led Him into a wilderness—forty days of fasting, solitude, and satanic attack. He faced hunger, temptation, and isolation.

"Then Jesus, being filled with the Holy Spirit, returned from the Jordan and was led by the Spirit into the wilderness." — Luke 4:1 (NKJV)

This was divine design. The Father was not absent—He was refining His Son's dependence. Jesus emerged from the wilderness in power because He had relied solely on the Word of God.

Lesson: The wilderness doesn't weaken the anointed—it sharpens them. If you can survive the dry place with only the Word, you can stand anywhere in the world.

GOD WILL REMOVE EVERY CRUTCH

To carry the anointing, you must walk without crutches. The support systems, voices, and comforts you once leaned on will be removed, not because they were wrong, but because God wants to be your source.

"And you shall remember the Lord your God, for it is He who gives you power to get wealth, that He may [a]establish

His covenant which He swore to your fathers, as it is this day." — Deuteronomy 8:18 (NKJV)

God will dry up brooks, close doors, and even allow relationships to shift—not to hurt you, but to position you. What you lose in the natural, you gain in spiritual authority.

Lesson: The anointed must be addicted to the presence of God—not addicted to provision or popularity.

THOSE WHO RELY ON GOD ARE NEVER EMPTY

When you learn to depend on God alone, you will never run dry. Like the widow with the oil and flour, obedience to God's instruction ensures supernatural supply—even in famine.

"The bin of flour was not used up, nor did the jar of oil run dry, according to the word of the Lord which He spoke by Elijah." — 1 Kings 17:16 (NKJV)

He will sustain you, not just physically, but emotionally, spiritually, and mentally. When you are emptied of all else, His presence becomes your portion.

REFLECTION QUESTIONS

- Is God currently stripping away your comforts to draw you closer?

- Are you trusting Him as your full source—or leaning on alternatives?

- What would it look like to be fully sustained by Him?

KEY TAKEAWAY

The truly anointed do not survive by natural means—they are sustained supernaturally. God will lead you to places where He alone can uphold you, so that your faith is unshakable, your power undeniable, and your dependence unmovable. When God is all you have, you will find He is more than enough.

CHAPTER ELEVEN

ANOINTED BUT MISUNDERSTOOD

"Is this not the carpenter, the Son of Mary, and brother of James, Joses, Judas, and Simon? And are not His sisters here with us?" So they were offended at Him. But Jesus said to them, "A prophet is not without honor except in his own country, among his own relatives, and in his own house."
— Mark 6:3–4 (NKJV)

WHEN YOUR CALLING OFFENDS THE FAMILIAR

There is a unique pain that comes with being anointed but misunderstood. When God places His hand on your life, those closest to you may not recognize it. They may question your calling, challenge your decisions, or criticize your obedience, not because you're wrong, but because you no longer fit the box they built for you.

To be anointed is to be set apart—and that separation often brings misunderstanding. The more deeply you walk with God, the more misunderstood you may become by people who once walked closely with you.

JESUS: THE REJECTED REDEEMER

Jesus, though the very Son of God, was rejected by those in His own hometown. He taught with wisdom, healed the sick, and cast out demons, yet familiarity bred contempt.

> **"Now He could do no mighty work there, except that He laid His hands on a few sick people and healed them. And He marveled because of their unbelief. Then He went about the villages in a circuit, teaching." — Mark 6:5–6 (NKJV)**

Their refusal to accept who He was cost them access to what He carried. But notice: *Jesus didn't stop being who He was just because they couldn't see it.*

Lesson: Their inability to discern your anointing doesn't diminish its reality. It only reveals their spiritual limitation.

DAVID: MISJUDGED BY HIS OWN FAMILY

When David arrived on the battlefield to check on his brothers, he was met with accusations rather than appreciation. His oldest brother Eliab said:

> **"Why did you come down here? And with whom have you left those few sheep in the wilderness? I know your pride and the insolence of your heart, for you have come down to see the battle." — 1 Samuel 17:28 (NKJV)**

David was misunderstood, not because he was arrogant, but because he carried something they couldn't comprehend. His anointing to defeat Goliath was invisible to those who only saw his youth.

Lesson: People who can't see what God placed in you will often reduce you to what they've always known about you.

HANNAH: MISUNDERSTOOD IN THE PLACE OF PRAYER

Hannah, desperate for a child, poured out her soul before the Lord in the temple. Yet instead of being met with compassion, she was accused by the high priest.

> **"How long will you be drunk? Put your wine away from you!" — 1 Samuel 1:14 (NKJV)**

Eli mistook deep intercession for drunkenness. Hannah wasn't wrong—she was anointed for birth, but the process looked messy and misunderstood.

Lesson: The deeper your travail, the more likely you are to be judged by shallow observers.

THE ANOINTING WILL SET YOU APART—AND APARTNESS INVITES SCRUTINY

To be anointed is to walk a different path. You won't always be able to explain your steps, justify your sacrifices, or articulate the fire burning within you. And that will make others uncomfortable.

> **"The wind blows where it wishes... So is everyone who is born of the Spirit." — John 3:8 (NKJV)**

The anointed are like the wind—led by the Spirit, uncontained by the expectations of men. But that freedom offends those bound by familiarity and tradition.

Lesson: You don't owe everyone an explanation, especially when your obedience looks like disobedience to those lacking discernment.

MISUNDERSTANDING IS THE PRICE OF OBEDIENCE

Sometimes, obedience will make you look irrational. When God tells you to walk away, build, launch, sow, wait, or confront, people will question your sanity. But what seems foolish in man's eyes is often divine in heaven's view.

> **"For the message of the cross is foolishness to those who are perishing…"** — **1 Corinthians 1:18a (NKJV)**

You are not called to be understood by everyone. You are called to be faithful to the voice of God, even when it costs you relationships, reputation, or comfort.

REFLECTION QUESTIONS

- Have you ever been deeply misunderstood because of your calling or obedience?

- Are you willing to be set apart, even if it means being misjudged?

- Do you find your validation in God's affirmation or man's approval?

KEY TAKEAWAY

Being anointed does not guarantee being accepted. In fact, the greater the anointing, the greater the chances of being misunderstood. But take heart—Jesus was misunderstood, and yet He fulfilled His purpose perfectly. Your assignment doesn't require their approval. Walk in what God said, even when others don't understand it.

CHAPTER TWELVE

THE GLORY AFTER THE GETHSEMANE

**"And being in agony, He prayed more earnestly... Then an angel appeared to Him from heaven, strengthening Him."
— Luke 22:44, 43 (NKJV)**

THERE IS GLORY, BUT FIRST—THERE IS GETHSEMANE

The Gethsemane experience is the ultimate place of surrender, agony, and crushing. It is the moment when your will collides with God's, and you're faced with the question: *Will I obey, even if it costs me everything?* Every anointed vessel must pass through this garden. There is no resurrection without crucifixion. No power without pressing. No glory without surrender.

Yet, there is glory after the Gethsemane. The garden is not the end—it is the gateway. What begins with anguish ends with glory, if we do not run from the process.

Jesus: The Anointed One in the Olive Press

Gethsemane means *"oil press."* It was the place where Jesus sweated drops of blood while His disciples slept. He wrestled with the weight of His assignment, asking:

"Father, if it is Your will, take this cup away from Me; nevertheless not My will, but Yours be done." — Luke 22:42 (NKJV)

This moment was not weakness—it was worship. It was obedience birthed through pain. Jesus, though sinless, had to choose surrender. The cross wasn't forced—it was embraced.

Lesson: The greatest anointing flows from the greatest surrender.

Gethsemane Separates the Called from the Chosen

Many are called, but few are chosen, because not everyone will stay in the garden. Some sleep through the press. Others run from the weight. But the chosen stay long enough to say yes, even through tears.

"Then all the disciples forsook Him and fled." — Matthew 26:56 (NKJV)

The anointed must sometimes walk alone. The deeper your yes, the fewer people can walk with you.

Lesson: Gethsemane is where God filters out distractions so your purpose becomes pure.

THE PRESSING PRODUCES STRENGTH

Though Jesus was in agony, something powerful happened in His surrender.

"Then an angel appeared to Him from heaven, strengthening Him." — Luke 22:43 (NKJV)

The strength to finish your assignment doesn't come before the crushing—it comes in it. God doesn't give you strength to escape Gethsemane; He gives you strength to endure it.

Lesson: The garden will not kill you. It will strip you, empty you, and refine you, but it will also strengthen you.

AFTER THE GARDEN COMES GLORY

After Gethsemane came the betrayal. After betrayal came the cross. After the cross came the grave. And after the grave came resurrection.

"Therefore God also has highly exalted Him and given Him the name which is above every name..." — Philippians 2:9 (NKJV)

The path to glory goes through humility, suffering, and death to self. But the glory is sure. Jesus didn't stay in Gethsemane. Neither will you.

There is oil for your obedience, power for your pressing, and glory on the other side of surrender.

GETHSEMANE IS THE FINAL TEST BEFORE THE RELEASE

Many people quit just before their breakthrough—because Gethsemane demands everything. It is not the place of comfort. It is the place of confrontation. Your calling is validated here, not by men, but by heaven.

When you endure Gethsemane, you step into your greatest authority, not because you're perfect, but because you're poured out.

"He poured out His soul unto death... and He bore the sin of many." — Isaiah 53:12 (NKJV)

Lesson: The oil that flows from your Gethsemane will minister to others in ways your gifting never could.

REFLECTION QUESTIONS

- Have you faced your Gethsemane moment yet?

- What part of your will is God asking you to surrender?

- Are you willing to endure the crushing for the glory that follows?

KEY TAKEAWAY

There is a Gethsemane for every anointed life—a place of deep surrender, internal struggle, and radical obedience. But Gethsemane is not your grave—it is your gateway. When you pass through it, strengthened by heaven and emptied of self, you will walk into the fullness of your calling. The cost is great, but the glory after the Gethsemane is greater.

CONCLUSION

THE PRICE IS HIGH, BUT THE OIL IS WORTH IT

"Therefore I remind you to stir up the gift of God which is in you through the laying on of my hands. For God has not given us a spirit of fear, but of power..." — 2 Timothy 1:6–7 (NKJV)

The anointing is not cheap. It is not casual. It is not convenient. It is costly.

To walk in the divine power, presence, and authority of God means you must first be willing to walk through pain, surrender, sacrifice, and fire. The anointing does not fall on the fleshly—it rests on the broken. It is not given to the popular—it is entrusted to the pure. It does not come through ambition—it is birthed through obedience.

As we've journeyed through each chapter, we have seen the real road that leads to the oil:

- You must answer the call—knowing it will cost.

- You must embrace brokenness as preparation for power.

- You must carry the mantle with reverence, knowing its weight.

- You must welcome solitude and separation as divine appointments.

- You must choose obedience over opportunity—every time.

- You must be hidden before you're honored.

- You must pass through the furnace of testing to be refined.

- You must endure the crushing that produces the oil.

- You must bear rejection and ridicule without losing your resolve.

- You must learn to be sustained by God alone.

- You must accept being misunderstood for the sake of the assignment.

- And ultimately, you must surrender in Gethsemane to walk in resurrection glory.

THE COST IS PERSONAL

No one can pay your price for you. No mentor, friend, or family member can carry your cross. The oil on your life will flow in proportion to your surrender. The deeper the crush, the purer the oil. The greater the pressure, the more weighty the presence. You cannot shortcut the process, because the process is what makes the anointing real.

THE ANOINTING IS SACRED

We are living in a generation where the external is often glorified—talent is celebrated, charisma is platformed, and appearance is praised. But God is still looking for anointed vessels. Not just gifted ones. Not just visible ones. Anointed ones—those who have paid the price in private and walk in purity, humility, and authority in public.

God is not impressed by your skillset; He is moved by your surrender. He does not anoint entertainers—He anoints servants.

THE REWARD IS ETERNAL

The reward for paying the price of the anointing is not popularity, promotion, or applause. The reward is His presence, His power, and His pleasure. It's the joy of walking with Him, of seeing lives transformed, of knowing heaven backs your obedience.

"You anoint my head with oil; my cup runs over." — Psalm 23:5 (NKJV)

The overflow comes after the oil. The impact flows after the crushing. The glory follows the Gethsemane.

FINAL CHALLENGE: WILL YOU PAY THE PRICE?

The question is not whether you want the anointing or not. The real question is: *Are you willing to pay the price to carry it?*

The Cost of the Anointing

Are you willing to go through what others run from?

Are you willing to be broken, crushed, and hidden?

Are you willing to endure misunderstanding, pain, and pressure—if it means more of Him?

If your answer is yes, then you are ready to walk into the sacred cost and call of the anointing.

May your life drip with fresh oil. May your prayers burn with holy fire. May your obedience thunder louder than the noise around you. And may you always remember: *The cost is great but the glory is greater.*

"But we have this treasure in earthen vessels, that the excellence of the power may be of God and not of us." — 2 Corinthians 4:7 (NKJV)

PRAYER OF CONSECRATION

Heavenly Father,

We come before You with reverence and humility, acknowledging that the anointing is not to be taken lightly. We thank You for the call You have placed upon our lives, and we recognize that with this call comes a cost. Lord, we do not seek position, applause, or recognition—we seek Your presence, Your power, and Your purpose.

Search our hearts, O God. Strip away every ounce of pride, selfish ambition, and spiritual complacency. Purify us as vessels of honor, ready to be used for Your glory. We surrender to the crushing, the pressing, and the refining, knowing that the oil that flows from brokenness is holy and precious in Your sight.

Give us the courage to walk the narrow road. Teach us to wait in hiddenness, to be faithful in the wilderness, and to obey You when it is inconvenient, uncomfortable, and costly. Let our lives be a continual offering upon the altar of Your will.

Father, we say "yes" to the process. We say "yes" to the fire. We say "yes" to the secret place, to the discipline, and to the consecration. Anoint us, not for fame, but for function. Not for show, but for service. Not for our names to be known, but for Your name to be lifted high.

May Your Spirit rest upon us in power and purity. May the oil that flows from our lives destroy yokes, heal the broken, and glorify Christ. Let Your anointing mark us, mold us, and move through us to accomplish all that You have ordained.

In Jesus' holy and anointed name, Amen.